THE NOBLE MAN

(The Human Virtues: The Necessity of Life)

THE NOBLE MAN

MAN

(The Human Virtues: The Necessity of Life)

JohnMary Edurumba

Copyright: JohnMary Edurumba

Email: omasirigod2016@gmail.com

Tel: 08127067022

Nihil Obstat

Rev. Fr. Dr. Patrick Paul Udoh

(Censor Deputatus, Archdiocese of Onitsha)

09/05/2016.

TABLE OF CONTENTS

ACKNOWLEDGEMENT

At the completion of this work, I profoundly thank God Almighty to whom I pray to every day of my life. Greatest thanks to the Mother of all graces, the Blessed Virgin Mary, the Mother of Our Saviour and my intercessor.

I thank heartily and sincerely to our father founder Francis Cardinal Arinze, for all his good works and innovation towards the growth and progress of our Congregation. My gratitude goes to Most Rev. Dr. Valerian M. Okeke, the Archbishop of Onitsha and his Auxiliary Bishop of Onitsha Most Rev. Dr. Denis Isizoh; I thank you heartily my Superior General Very Rev. Br. Pantaleon Okafor, for being always available with listening ears and to the entire Brother's of St. Stephen Congregation and equally thank my Co-Religious brothers they are, Valentine Obiora, Romanus Ude, Augustine Eze, Paul Amaku, Theophilus Egbu-ulu, MacJulian Onyejegbu, Johnmary Edurumba and Paul Azigba.

My gratitude goes to Rev. Brothers: Paul Ezennamezi, Chijioke Nnanyelugo BSS, Thomas B. Abonyi MJ and Vincent Orakwe BSS. I equally thank Rev. Sisters: Edith Nnolum DCPC, Mary John Vianney Ezechukwu IHM, Evelyn Muonanu DLL, Catherine Umewuzie SPEA, Chibundu Omeokache IHM, Chizoba Ozokwere DMMM, Euphemia Okoroama MSDM, Chidiamara AnigboguDLL, Chidimma NnajiMSDM, Mary Constantia Aniekwe IHM, Georgian Akubueze CM, and Veronica C. ukomadu, they are my companions and being always at my side.

I profoundly thank Rev. Fr. Dr. Patrick Paul Udoh, who granted the Nihil Obstat, and I thank also Rev. Fr. Dr. Marius Obiagwu, the Parish Priest of the Holy Spirit Parish Omagba and also Rev. Fathers Evalistus Nwagbala, Anthony Nzomiwu, Henri Duru CM, Raphael Uzoekwe CMF, Patrick Unegbu, Modestus UzoekweCSSP, Clement Kafor CM, Vincent Obi, Chrysanthus Igwe, Innocent Egbunike and Brother (Monk) Cyril O. Ejezie OCSO, for their fatherly encouragement to me, may Almighty God continuously protect and guide you all in His vineyard in Jesus name, Amen.

Special thanks to you Rev. Fr. Dr. Joebarth Chiemeka Abba, a prolific writer, for all his encouragement and innovation, May God continue to bless you in all your endeavours. And I want to sincerely thank these people who also did wonderfully in editing this work like Mrs Chidinma Uzoma, she is kind and a mother to me, Sir Ignatius Nduka, my Principal at Army Day Sec, School, Onitsha, Mr. Ifeanyi Nzekwu, my lecturer in College of Education Nsugbe and Mirabel O. Orieoma, may God continuously bless and protect you all in your various needs. And a deep gratitude to you Mr Njubigbo C. N, my English teacher at Army Day Sec, School, Onitsha, who also critically proof–read and wrote the forward for this book and took it as his own, may God in His infinite goodness bless you and your family.

My gratitude goes to Rev. Fathers: Dr. Emmanuel Egwuoba, Edwin Udoye, Joseph Ezeugo, Callistus

Mbanwusi, James Obiaju, Augustine Nweke, Ike Muoma and Henry Okenu. I equally thank Rev. Brothers:RomanusIgwurubeBSS, Anthony EzeBSS, Gabinus Afuecheta BSS, Denis Omem BSS, Joseph Chukwuakpu BSS, Livinus Walter BSS and Joseph Igboekwene MJ.

I sincerely thank Dr. (Mrs) Kate O. Ezeoba, my lecturer in College of Education Nsugbe, Mrs Rose Okpala, my Vice Principal at Army Day Sec, School, Onitsha, Mr Innocent P.C. Okoye, Mr & Mrs Edwin A. Okoye, Mr Romanus Nwankwo and Onyinye Okeke, may God in His infinite goodness guide you all in your various need.I acknowledge the authors and some other individuals whom few of their Booklets were looked into.

This basket of thanks will be incomplete if I do not mention my immediate family members, uncles and family friends who are always by my side. They are; Mr & Mrs Nestor Nzekwe, Hon. John Nwokeji(Tallest), Mr Januarius Maduabuchi, Mr Ekene Obieli, Mr Enestmartin Udabagu,

Mrs Abigail Edurumba, Mrs Stella Aji, Mrs Rita Ilongwo, Florence Okonkwo, Mrs Ifeoma Umunna, Mrs Chinwe Ezeanusiobi, Mrs Theresa Etuke, Mr & Mrs Ifeanyi Edurumba, Mr & Mrs Donatus Uzoanakwe, Hyginus Aji, Engr. Okwuoha, Mr & Mrs Humphrey Uzoma, Mr Alphonsus and Mrs Ijeoma Ifediba, Tina Mary Agudiegwu, Mrs Gertrude Mary Onyeche, Mrs Judith Obi, , Mrs Assumpta Ejimnkeonye, Mrs Martina Nweke, Anthonia Okeke, AfomaEzeoba, Chika Obi, Martha Okeke, Chinaza Onuegbu, Alphonsus Obi and EzenetoC. Amara, may God bless, protect and reward you all abundantly.

To all who contributed in one way or the other to the production of this booklet, may Almighty God bless and replenish you all abundantly in Jesus name, Amen.

(KaChukwuna – eduunu ma nonyereunuoge nine!)

FORWARD

The Noble Man is JohnMary Vianney ample work on the Virtues of the Noble Man. In his words, the noble man is one who has the behaviour of showing the highest moral standard, moral excellence, positive trail or quality demanded to be morally good.

His efforts to provide such sound book on this topic is therefore most recommendable. The book to my mind is a must-read for everybody, the young, and the old and for schools and other organizations that wish to inculcate values like humility, strong will, ethical principles and uprightness.

I ask you to invest in the book because investing in a good is a right step in a right direction as Plato said, "It is better to be unborn than to be untaught". Roosevelt corroborated and said, "Knowledge Governs Ignorance".

I plead with you to devote time to read through this book because that is the only way you will find what will influence you for good and also discover what you may like to challenge, positively any way.

Njubigbo C. N.

Dedication

In Thanksgiving to God for Mr and Mrs Nestor Nzekwe,
on their 25thyears of Marriage Anniversary

INTRODUCTION

A noble person is someone who is virtuous and to be virtuous entails a habit or firm disposition which inclines a person to do good and avoid evilfor his/her neighbour. It is characterized by stability. A virtuous person not only strives to be a good person, but also seeks what is good and chooses to act in a good way. Virtue is that which makes both a person and what he/she does good.

On one hand, an individual can acquire human virtues through his/her own effort under the guidance of reason. Through education, by deliberately choosing to do what is good, and through perseverance, a person acquires and strengthens virtues.

On the other hand, with the help of Divine Grace the individual finds greater strength and facility to practise these virtues. Through these grace-assisted virtues, which we would now call 'moral virtues', the person gains self-mastery of his/her self.

CHAPTER ONE

The Virtuous Noble Man

A noble person is a virtuous man and virtue here means goodness. He is one who has the behaviour of showing the highest moral standard, moral excellence, positive trait or quality deemed to be morally good. The noble person is thus valued as a foundation of principle and good moral being.

We still have such people in our societies. They have the habitual and firm dispositions to do good. It is always such persons that champion positive developments in our communities. Where there are no electricity, good drinking water, health centers, schools, roads, etc. they provide them. They are always there, contributing to the positive development of their societies.

Being a noble person is to know when and how to act accordingly while still keeping your dignity and values in place. It takes everything you stand for, whether others approve of it or not, and putting it to use to make your surroundings a better place, not only for you, but for others. Being a noble person, as mentioned above is indeed a requirement in society.

The possessive characteristics of a noble person

➢ Standing up for what he believes in.
➢ Upholding his personal and moral values.
➢ Living life for others.

The Virtues of a Noble Person

These are some virtues which a noble person should possess: courage, truth, honour, fidelity, discipline, hospitality, industry, self – reliance, and perseverance.

COURAGE

The word, courage, comes from the Latin word "Animus" and it basically means that one is brave. One can be brave physically, which means that one is willing to fight for what one believes is right. For example, one might defend someone who is being hurt by a person who is bigger or stronger than him/her.

Another kind of courage is called moral courage. It means standing up for what one believes, even when it would be easier to keep quiet. Supposing someone uses words that put someone down because of one's skin colour, religion, or parent's background. If one speaks up and says that people should be judged by what they do, not on how they look or what they believe, one is practising the noble virtue of courage. If one hears someone tell a lie that could hurt someone else, and one calls him to order, one is acting with courage. Courage also means doing what one believes that is right, or refusing to do what one believes that is wrong. Even when other people laugh at you and friends won't support your choice, practising courage is good in life. Let's practise it.

Importance of Courage: Almost everyone understands what being brave is all about. However, an important thing to know is that being brave doesn't mean that one is not afraid. What makes people courageous is doing the right thing even when they are afraid. Another important idea is that being brave doesn't mean that one should misbehave. If one sees someone being beaten up by a person who is too big for one to fight without getting hurt yourself, one uses one's courage to find an adult to stop the fight. Courage is the virtue that gives one the heart to do the best one can do to defend others and to do what is right.

TRUTH

The virtue of truth sounds very simple. It basically means that you don't tell lies. However, there is more to practising truth than that. *For example, the easiest way to avoid telling lies is never do anything that you aren't comfortable telling people about*. You need to be honest yourself, too. *Don't give yourself excuses for doing things that you believe are wrong which make them sound as if they are okay*. You don't make stealing right by saying that no one will miss what you take. Telling lies so that you won't be punished for doing something you know you shouldn't have done, makes what you did worse, not better. Part of practising truth is having the courage to always owe up to what you did.

Importance of Truth: Probably the important thing to know about practicing the truth is that not everyone agrees about what is truth. Sometimes things that seem to contradict each other can both be true. If you really believe that something is true, you don't have to make other people agree with you. You are only responsible for yourself. Perhaps the people you disagree with know something you don't know and may not be ready to see what you did see. Good friends can agree to disagree on lots of things without having quitting being friends.

HONOUR

The basic meaning of honour is respect. When you honour people, you express your feelings that they have earned respect for a particular action or for the way they live their lives. Your personal sense of honour is your commitment to live by the standards you believe should earn you respect from others. All the virtues are part of practising honour. If you act with courage, tell the truth, be loyal to others, behave with discipline, be hospitable and industrious, rely on yourself to accomplish things, and persevere until you finish what you set out to do, you will certainly command honour from others. If you live that way, you can honour and respect yourself as well and never need to be ashamed of what you have done.

Importance of Honour: You practise honour by respecting people's rights and beliefs and by keeping to your word. You also practise honour by making others respect your rights and keep their word to you. Honour means treating others the way you want to be treated and also getting in their faces when they don't treat you or your friends with respect. Most important of all in practising honour is keeping your promises. Therefore it means that you have to think before you make a promise. If you're not sure you can do something you are asked to do, it is okay for you to say that you try your possible best but aren't sure you can deliver. It's not okay to say a word without keeping the promise.

FIDELITY

Fidelity is just a big word for being faithful or loyal to a person or a group of people or to an idea. *For example, if your friend is being teased by others in a way that makes him or her feel bad, fidelity is standing by your friend, defending your friend, and refusing to join in the tease, no matter what*. If you believe that it's important to tell the truth. You practise fidelity by never telling a lie. Obeying the laws of your community is one way to practice fidelity. If someone in your family is in trouble, you try to help him/her out if you can, even if you don't agree with what got him into trouble. However, fidelity does not include doing something you know is wrong in order to give them that help.

Rules of Fidelity: The important part in practising fidelity is to be careful about who you give your loyalty to. If you belong to a group that thinks it is good to use harmful drugs or to lie to their parents, your being faithful to the group could also mean breaking the law or behaving dishonourably. If a group you belong to does not support your doing what is right, you need to withdraw your loyalty and get out of the group. That's part of practising fidelity also, being faithful to your own belief.

DISCIPLINE

The word, discipline, originally comes from a word that meant teaching and learning. The idea was that when you teach, you put out a pattern of knowledge or behaviour that students fit in for. The basic idea is that there are patterns of life that are worth learning to fit in. Also the essence of learning is to change your behaviour to fit in to such patterns. For example, the best way to stay healthy is to learn the pattern of eating healthy meals and exercising which creates a strong body, then practise fidelity to that pattern. All the virtues are part of discipline, a pattern of thinking and acting which you practise until they are so much part of who you are; that they almost define who you are. Discipline sometimes seems to mean something unpleasant, like when a parent disciplines or punishes a child to teach the child how to behave. Because of many forms of punishment when you fail to match the pattern, many people think discipline is an unpleasant thing. It depends on how you look at it. For example, dancers may work very hard and even experience pain to learn a particular dance, but the reward is the pleasure of creating the beauty of the dance, both for the performer and the audience. The trick in practising discipline is to choose to learn and practise patterns that make you or your life better, so that the end result is worth any trouble the process may create.

Importance of Discipline: The most important aspect of discipline that you practise is self – discipline, that is, you decide you want to match a pattern and then you keep working at making the pattern a part of how you live until it is part of your character. For example, if you can make eating a right meals and exercising so much a part of your life that you are uncomfortable, if you are not leaving that pattern, you are much more likely to live a long life and to be healthy even when you are very old.

HOSPITALITY

Hospitality is the virtue where you recognize that in addition to being an individual, you are also part of a community. Hospitality means opening your house to travellers and treating people who come to visit you with the same kindness and respect as you give your own family members. The idea is that humans survive by helping oneanother and in that way all humans are parts of the same family. You practise hospitality when you treat other people like they are your family, with kindness and respect.

Ways to Show Hospitality: We no longer live in a world where you can comfortably invite strangers into your home. You can still do other things, though, like treating strangers with courtesy, helping people in your community, by helping with food supplies for the poor and other projects like neighbourhood cleanup, and house repair for disabled people, helping children cross the roads and safely, or helping a friend get settled in a new house. Hospitality is also making your friends and relatives feel at home when they come to your house, and perhaps offering them something to eat or drink. The other side of hospitality is behaving well when you are a guest in someone else's home. It might mean avoiding a fight with your cousin or helping the younger children get something to eat at a family gathering. In general, if you treat other people the way you would like to be treated, you are practising hospitality.

INDUSTRIOUS

Basically, industrious means hard-working, persistence; or working to accomplish something. It also means doing more than the least you can to meet up with others. If you have a job, do the best you know how to do and take pride in doing it right, whether or not people notice that you do more than you have to. If someone asks you to do a job and you accept the responsibility, they can count on you to complete it, do it on time and meet the standards they set. You practise being industrious by how well you work. In the same way that you try to get most work done for the time and effort you put in a job, so should you try to play so as to have most fun and most joy in living.

Importance of being Industrious: The idea behind the virtue of industry is to be wholehearted in whatever you do, to get the most you can from the time and effort you spend. How you judge depends on what is important and enjoyable to you. What do you think is more industrious to do? Watching TV, reading good books, watching a football game, dancing to a music video? To suggest: there aren't the right answers. You choose what is most valuable to you, to make you industrious in life.

SELF – RELIANCE

Another word for self – reliance is responsibility, especially for you. As much as you can, you need to be independent of the help of others. For example, if you're supposed to go to a football practice, don't count on your mother to remind you No, you should notice what time it is, and be ready when it's time to go for that practice. Another way to be self-reliant is to find ways to get the things you want by earning money or trading on things rather than always expecting your parents to get them for you. It also means 'clean up' when you make a mess. Being self-reliant does not mean that you don't get help from others. It just means that you do what you can for yourself, and only ask others for things you can't do – like drive a car or solve a really difficult mathematical problem. On the mathematical problems, you need to try hard before you give up and ask for help.

Importance of Self – Reliance: As you grow older, there are more and more things you can do for yourself. Practising self-reliance means that you learn to do those things, so you don't have to depend on other people so much. It also means that when other people need help, you give to them in such a way that they would be able to do for themselves the next time.

PERSEVERANCE

Perseverance is the virtue of keeping on until you finish the job. It's easy to get discouraged about projects, because all projects have places where it looks like you're never going to get through them. In fact, sometimes, you just fall on your face and make a mess. Practising perseverance means getting up and trying again or trying another way to do what has to be done. On the other hand, if what you're trying to do is not worth your time and effort, you don't get credit for being stupid in life. A lot of people have special talents, but people who "keep on, keep in." and would always do better than talented people who don't persevere.

Importance of Perseverance: The best combination of all is to persevere in learning how to use your special talents and in learning new skills and abilities. No one can beat a combination of ability and perseverance. And if you fail sometimes, that's okay, because it's okay for you to make mistakes you need to persevere. It is the people who fail and get fast through their failure that really succeed in life.

In conclusion, the life of a noble person is good and deserving, that is the life of a virtuous person. It is worthy to start such good life early in life. The life of virtue helps one to become successful in whatever one chooses to do. Besides, who wouldn't want to have these virtues of a noble person? I am sure no one would like to be left out.

CHAPTER TWO

The Features Of Human Virtue

The human virtue is the firm foundation upon which a full and worthy life is built. Human virtue also called natural virtue, helps us to become human and orient us towards the true, the good and the beautiful. It lays the foundation for meaningful and selfless relationship with one another. Human virtue lays the foundation for a loving relationship with God (It is supplemented through grace by another set of virtues called "the supernatural virtues", which help us to love). There are four virtues that are considered 'hinges' upon which all other virtues turn. They are Prudence, Justice, Fortitude and Temperance. They are called the 'Cardinal Virtues'; these firm habits are connected to all other human virtues as well as to the supernatural virtues.

"The Human virtue is characterized with firm attitudes, stable disposition, habitual perfections of intellect should that govern our actions, order our passions, and guide our conducts according to reason and faith. The virtue makes one to be self-mastering,

and joy in leading a morally good life. The virtuous man is he who freely practises the good".

"The moral virtues are acquired by human efforts. They are the fruit and seed of morally good acts; they dispose all the powers of the human beings for communion with divine love". (CCC. 1804).

Why We Practise Virtue

Virtuous living is a basic quality of life and necessary for our well being and happiness. It is necessary because when we practise virtue and build ourselves in it, we progress, we will attract what we may have been missing in our lives such as fulfilling relationships, achievement of meaningful goals, happiness, and so on.

The moment we declare, "I am persevering to achieve this goal in spite of all obstacles, self – doubt and fear", a move occurs where we naturally become more focused, determined, and courageous, leading us to success. Virtue is good to practise and live by it in life.

Some Basic Characteristics of Virtue

Virtues are dispositional features of character. They make us good and make us do our jobs well. They affect our character, and our lives. Therefore, we can predict how a person possessing the virtue will act and react in different situations. Someone who acquires honesty is an honest person; honesty disposes this person to act honestly.

Virtues are voluntarily acquired: We are not born with them; it is up to us to acquire them. As they are beneficial to us, we have as well reason to acquire them.

Virtues involve acting with judgment,they blend emotion and judgment.They are emotional perceptiveness, involving hitting the target, in the right way, at the right time, and so on. Courage is the blending of reason with fear, so that we learn to respond appropriately to our feelings of fear, maybe to run when appropriate, and to stand when we should.

Virtues are needed for living well. Without virtue, our lives would be spoilt. No one would choose a life without the virtues.

Virtues are pervasively relevant to all roles in life. Success at any project in life will require moderating our fear appropriately, being honest with ourselves, being fair, objective, and so on. Virtue is needed to achieve our aim while on earth.

Virtue involves acting with a proper motive: You cannot exercise virtue with a wrong motive. Some motives, like greed, malice, spite, envy, are completely incompatible with virtue.

CHAPTER THREE

The Attributes Of A Virtuous Human Being

The qualities that people would name when they describe you are what characterize a human being. It could be good or bad and makes you a person who is different from anyone else on earth. If your morality causes you to do good even when you might rather do something else, you are said to have a good character. If you make the same kind of acceptable choices, and don't let other people talk you into things that you believe are wrong, you are said to have a strong character.

Major Sorts of Character

None of us is still the same person we were some years back. We all change, some for better, some for worse. It is the same with characters, they move on as we progress, but the way in which they move on usually falls into one of these three major categories: change, growth, and fall.

The Change – This is our good old self, which basically transforms. This transformation is quite radical, despite some inner traits that is always within us.

The Growth – On this stage, a person overcomes an internal opposition of weakness, fear, and the past, while he faces an external opposition, and as a result he becomes a fuller and better person.

The Fall– Commonly known as a tragedy, the fall follows the person as he dooms himself or others.

CHAPTER FOUR

The Noble Leader

A noble leader is a person of good character who inspires and motivates others to achieve a common goal through trust and communication. He/she is 'a leader who exhibits superiority of not only mind, but also of character and morals'.

Noble leaders are different from traditional leaders or some other leaders in five ways: in his/her seeing, thinking, feeling, being and acting/doing.

1) A Noble Leader **SEES** a different. This includes to see: possibilities, not just problems, the good in people, not just their weaknesses.

2) ANoble Leader **THINKS** differently. He/she has a every big vision and goals, but little problems. What's right in any situation, rather than what is expedient. Profits as just one objective and measure, not be all end all.

3) A Noble Leader **FEELS** differently. What motivates him/her is different: A deeply-held sense of purpose, why we're in business – and coming to work. Forming more powerful relationships with people in the business.

4) A Noble Leader is different in his/her very **BEING**: He values being totally present with whomever he is working with. Holding higher values.

5) A Noble Leader **ACTS** differently: Maybe the noble leader takes different action, but it is because his/her actions are in line with morale and also above all, that those actions are much more powerful and effective.

NOTE: The Leader who does all five of the above is the one who rises to Noble Leadership.

WHERE THE NOBLE LEADER EXCELS

Being a noble leader, one must be a role model, knowledgeable in his/her field, and worthy of respect. There are many ways to lead people, whether it is by taking on a leadership role at work,in the family, at school. Here are some tips to help you excel as a noble leader in any situation in life.

1) The Noble Leader In An Environment

A noble leader in an environment is the person who has the most positive influence in life, and also has willingness to recognize the limitations of his own cultural norms, accept and adapt to the culture of that environment. The noble leader motivates an organization by creating a unique climate through selective leadership styles, also responsible for creating the vision and setting the direction for the future prosperity of that organization.

A noble leader needs to impact a vision providing focus to an organization. A successful leader in an environment or an organization is a servant to the people; servant leaders have positive impact on their organizations by adopting a good style of leadership, building emotional bonds with the focus that people come first.

He is to be a role model – To earn respect, it's important to show that you know your "stuff", to know whom you are and what you are up to do in your field. People will respect and listen to you, if they know you are knowledgeable in your field.

> ➢ Discuss your experience. Without showing off, let your employees understand how long you've been in the business and what you have achieved while you are there. Not only will they have a better understanding of why you're sitting in the boss' chair, but they would be more excited to be a part of your team and will admire you.
>
> ➢ Act professionally. Though you may be the leader, you should still be cordial to all your employees. You should also still meet the basic standards of professionalism such as; dressing appropriately,

coming to work and meetings on time, and communicating in a professional manner.

Leave room for input – Though it's important to be firm, you should still leave some room for the considerations of others. Through this way you won't look a dictator. Also, there's a lot you can learn from your employees, which might help your business thrive.

➢ Ask for feedback. It's important to ask for feedback after you've wrapped up a project, set up guideline during a meeting, or you have thrown a charity event. You can do this without scaring your employees. Simply ask through email, or send an anonymous survey to them.

➢ Ask for opinions in face-to-face situations. At the end of a meeting, you can casually ask if people have any questions or opinions. This will give your employees time to consider what they're working on. You may also pull individual employees aside, or invite them to your office, to discuss the project further. Tell them that their perspective is crucial to your success.

2) The Noble Teacher

The noble teacher in an institution is a well learned person who cares and values the personality of every person around him or her. He or she is an expert in the field where he or she has a course to teach.

How to Be a Noble Teacher

Show your expertise in the subject matter – It is important for your students to know that they can trust you as an expert in your field.

> ➢ When you introduce yourself, tell them how long you've been working in your field and what you have achieved there. Then they'll know that you know what you are in that field of yours.
> ➢ Tell them how long you've been teaching your course. If you've been teaching the same course for

five or ten years, let them know, so they will see you as a mentor.

> If you're new to the classroom, however, don't let your students know about it, so that they don't see you as one who is new in his/her field.

Establish your rules on first day – Once the introductions are done, it's important for you to let your students understand your expectations so that they can meet them.

> Have a well-organized syllabus that shows them exactly what to expect everyday of the course. Answer all questions they have so that you can clear up any confusion.

> Whether you're teaching children or adults, it's important to have a clear code of conduct, which shows not only your expectations, but the punishments.

*Common code of conducts include showing mutual respect and avoiding disruptive behaviours, such as, talking on the phone, or whispering at the back of the classroom.

Be a creative teacher – To be a noble teacher in the classroom, one need to have a new ways of introduces his/her subject to the students. If you don't mix things up, your students will get bored, distracted and may even lose respect for you.

➢ Bring current events into class discussions. Even if you're not teaching history as a course in the classroom, you can find a way to bring current materials, whether it's something related to the government or sports, tie them into your material. This will make your students feel that your discussion is relevant to the real world.

➢ Have unique activities that get your students moving and thinking. Allow your students to create their own ideals and how to manage them when they are in the real world.

Show your students that you care for them – To be a noble teacher in the classroom, you have to prove that you care about your students' success. Be kind and approachable in the classroom, so they respect you but aren't afraid to ask questions.

> ➤ Give good feedbacks on both written assignments as well as your students' in-class responses. This will show that you care about them on an individual level and want them to succeed.

> ➤ Thank them for a great class. On the last day of class, bring them a special treat, or write a note to say how much you've enjoyed having them in the classroom. This will make your classroom experience end on a positive note and will show what a great teacher you are.

3) Being The Noble Head Of Your Family

The noble head and provider in the family is to show love over the family. The noble head in the family is a person who sees that all matters in the home are solved, both physical and spiritual; Spiritual leadership in the family comprises home Bible studies and prayers. Again, the noble head in the family will be the 'breadwinner', works to make money to support the family.

Establish yourself as an authority figure – Make it clear that you are the man of your household, and that your rules should be followed.

- ➢ Demonstrate to your children that the elders should be respected at all times. If your parents play an active role in your life, you can show your children that you respect your parents, just as they should respect you.
- ➢ You should tell your children to treat you with respect. Because you are a figure of authority and should be addressed and answered appropriately, even during tense situations.

Have useful systems of rewards and punishments – In order to be the head of your household, your children should be aware that they will be rewarded for good behaviour and punished for not meeting your expectations.

➢ Have a reward for every successful occasions in your house.

➢ If your child did well in school, or reached an important milestone, such as a birthday, it's important to celebrate the occasion or any other way to your child's favourite destination, it will help to show that you care, and that you want him or her to keep succeeding.

The noble duty and responsibilities of every family member – In the family everyone has a role to play.

➢ The duties of the parent is to provide food, love, clothes, shelter and guidance,

➢ The duties of any child in the family is to be obedient, assist the household in any needs, and child care, to do well in school and prepare for a meaningful adulthood.

➢ The most important duties of parent is that of raising up a child. It is the most important because the child has to be raised from childhood till he/she reaches adult enough to take care of himself/herself.

CHAPTER FIVE

Punctuality: A Virtue Of A Noble Man

Punctuality is doing something at the time fixed for it. Also it's the characteristic of being able to complete a required task or fulfil an obligation before or at previously designated time. Sometimes we say "time waits for nobody". This has a lot to reactivate in the minds of some people of our generation who decorate their rooms with expensive wall clocks and adorn themselves with golden or silver wrist watches, without for once taken the pains to conform their lives to be conscious of time.

It is the secret of success in life. Most of the great men and women in the world are known for their punctuality. They know the value of time, and use it properly. They are aware of the fact that time does not wait for anyone. One should make the best use of time. Punctuality can help one to utilize one's time properly. A punctual person considers every work as important. He keeps his goodwill. By being punctual, he is disciplined, too. He can be trusted with any kind of responsibility.

A person who is not punctual to activities misses many things in life. He/she is not generally relied on by people for performing responsible job. For having a habit contrary to punctuality, he/she is likely to miss his/her bus, train or flight, or a business appointment or deal that could fetch him/her benefit. We should form a sense of punctual habit from our childhood, for our own benefit in future life.

Being punctual to our activities is one of the best ways of making good use of our time. It affects everyday activities of our life. Every human being has the same amount of time but the difference lies in its utility. Some use it for good while some misuse it. Those who make good use of their time will continue to reap the fruits until they die. But those who misuse theirs will live to regret it. It is appalling when some of us hold meetings or some will schedule a programme for a particular time and begin it after one hour without cogent reasons and apologies. What they normally say is "African Time". The Western time is not different from African time; the problem lies in the mindset of African people.

This generation does not value time factor. We should value time and be punctual in our various duties. Being punctual in your duty makes you orderly, disciplined and progressive in life.

Importance of punctuality

Being punctual is best in life and once we form the habit of time consciousness, it extends to everything we do.

➢ Punctuality is the most important characteristics of all successful people. The students, the officials, the traders, and lay-men, all have to observe punctuality in order to win glory and success in life.

➢ Punctuality brings in its trail efficiency. It may make or mar a career. If we look at the lives of all great men and women, we would realize that they had got a time schedule for everyday.

➢ Punctuality is a virtue which is doubly blessed. It impacts efficiency and keeps a man fit and healthy. If we get up early in the morning and take a walk everyday and follow a set-programme of life everyday, we shall be able to keep fit and healthy. But if we waver and show laxity in our daily programmes, we are bound to meet with failure in life.

Finally in punctuality, we can see that seasons change according to a set time-table, like the moon and the stars appear at a particular time. Thus everything in nature appears at a proper time. Nature teaches us to be punctual. If we follow the course of nature, we will keep fit, healthy and strong. No school, college or institution can function if punctuality is not observed there. Then punctuality is an important ingredient of all successful people. Punctuality implies maintaining regularity in our daily schedule of work. Punctuality is the gate-way to success.